THE TREES
WITNESS
EVERYTHING

THE TREES WITNESS EVERYTHING

VICTORIA CHANG

COPPER CANYON PRESS

PORT TOWNSEND, WASHINGTON

Cover design: Phil Kovacevich

Copper Canyon Press is in residence at Fort Worden
State Park in Port Townsend, Washington, under the
auspices of Centrum.
Centrum is a gathering place for artists and creative
thinkers from around the world, students of all ages
and backgrounds, and audiences seeking extraordinary
cultural enrichment.

LIBRARY OF CONGRESS
CATALOGING-IN-PUBLICATION DATA

Names: Chang, Victoria, 1970– author.
Title: The trees witness everything / Victoria Chang.
Description: Port Townsend, Washington :
Copper Canyon Press, [2022] |
Summary: "A collection of poems by
Victoria Chang"— Provided by publisher.
Identifiers: LCCN 2021053290 (print)
| LCCN 2021053291 (ebook)
| ISBN 9781556596322 (paperback)
| ISBN 9781619322516 (epub)
Subjects: LCGFT: Poetry.
Classification: LCC PS3603.H3575 T74 2022 (print) |
LCC PS3603.H3575
(ebook) | DDC 813/.6—dc23
LC record available at https://lccn.loc.gov/2021053290
LC ebook record available at
https://lccn.loc.gov/2021053291

9 8 7 6 5 4 3 2

COPPER CANYON PRESS

Post Office Box 271
Port Townsend, Washington 98368

www.coppercanyonpress.org

TO W.S. MERWIN

CONTENTS

I

II

III

IV

THE TREES
WITNESS
EVERYTHING

FAR ALONG IN THE STORY

Once I sat in rain,
opened my mouth to the sky.
I yearned to be changed.
But each drop was a small knife.
At first I fainted,
but when I woke up, all the
ticking had gone and
all the centuries were one.
My choices no longer hurt.

LOSING A LANGUAGE

We were born with a
large door on our backs. When will
we know if it opens?

GREEN FIELDS

I was supposed to
return to the fields daily.
I haven't been there
since birth. On some nights, I smell
smoke that I think is
God calling me, but when I
follow, there's just a
clothesline with half a life clipped
on it, drying in the sun.

CONVENIENCE

Youth stretches over
everything, can be used once.
Then we turn it inside out.

THE COLD BEFORE THE MOONRISE

The moon is alone,
always in the first person.
The days are dark. When
it shines on my face, it leaves
white scribbles. I used to think
the moon was illiterate.

HORSES

The way their eyes stare,
sometimes I wonder if we
are really hollow inside.

FIRST SIGHT

I see an outline
of you everywhere I look.
We spend our lives trying to
see our insides. Have
you ever watched the trees turn
black before the sky?

PROPHECY

I want to believe
that each of us has a note.
That at the end of the year,
the stars do turn off.
There's so much suffering, but
ask for proof and I have none.

SNOWFALL

We say the snow falls,
but it really seizes.
Because it is light,
it takes seven years to grab.
By the time it does,
the old wars are over and
my mother is dead.
But it lands on the new wars,
melts on a different mother.

STILL MORNING

No mornings are still.
The newly dead move the most.
They force flowers to dilate.

WHEN YOU GO AWAY

I look at my hands,
watch how they bend, just like air,
can sit still like ice,
the small lines at the knuckles,
how they can drag hair,
or cover a woman's mouth.
I should have kept the
ashes of her hands to see
whether they could still be held.

TO THE BOOK

Here is March again.
An image is a shawl. Birds
are a transcript of our thoughts.

NEWS OF THE ASSASSIN

The reporters are
busy interviewing bees,
filming footage of
their team meetings to survive.
Things are killed each day.
We walk away from mirrors,
close windows to rain.
Each day, a woman's thoughts die—
we pin them to a man's mind.

THE FLIGHT

I no longer watch
the birds during the day. I
prefer to save them
for my dreams where an owl's face
has more than one expression.

TO ASHES

How many ashes
do I walk through in one day?
I have forgotten
where my mother's ashes are.
I think they are flushed
into the earth. Yesterday,
the crow gave me an
invoice for its signaling
of death—I owe one whole year.

AVOIDING NEWS BY THE RIVER

All the announcements.
The mayflies land on a leaf.
No one there ever looks up.

THE OLD ROOM

Whose hands do I have?
The general from the Union,
the child dead of mumps,
the girl who died on her back,
the man over her?
The past is never finished,
the future is scared.
What if we aren't descendants
of anyone but ourselves?

THANKS

Some days I can't see
beyond the two small lemons
as they pull down the branches.

THE SHORTEST NIGHT

And when I looked up,
the sky had also turned black
and I had aged a
hundred more feet down the road.
The owl was on the
next tree with mirrors as eyes,
in case I wanted
to see my future. When I
looked, I lost another year.

ANCESTRAL VOICES

I hate my own voice,
but someone after me will
wonder if it was
threadbare or if its tiny
wings made noises when I slept.

PASSING

Someone said, at first
we want romance, then for life
to be bearable,
at last, understandable.
I am frightened, now
that the trees look like question
marks, how the moon makes
strange noises but it's daytime.
Bells have begun to notice me.

HISTORY

Today is circling,
history is transparent,
the future has no insides.

RAIN LIGHT

When the mothers leave,
what are we supposed to do?
I have rented light,
but all that's left is a search-
light shining in the
wrong country. What happens to
those raindrops now that
someone has seen them?

GIFT

Is silence a gift?
I can't hear my bones shrinking,
the lemon turning yellow.
The flag is louder
than my memories. How I
wish time were a wooden wheel.

THE THREAD

Once I thought the thread
was God so I've held the string
like a leash, thinking
that one day it would pull me
toward light. But what
if it's just a string, all the
seasons just dresses,
things to put on and take off.

NO ONE

A church is empty.
Where are all the secrets?
Under the pew is a plum.

FLY

What happened to the
eagle that lost its wing and
lived in the small cage,
feral like silence.
We stood there with our futures,
filming with our phones.
I wonder if the bird felt
me replay it on the plane.

INVOCATION

Five days, five nights, or
was it three skies and four fields?
Your mouth was a hole.
I never bothered to look.
Now that you are dead, I look—
there was nothing but language.

THE RIVER OF BEES

There are no more bees.
Remember how they glided?
Don't worry, they are not dead.
They have flown past death.
There, they walk on two legs,
build their hives out of concrete.

ORIOLES

When the lights are off,
I can imagine the orange,
their wings sound like men.
They only eat ripe fruit,
uninterested in humans.

ANOTHER YEAR COME

Suddenly I am
free from everything but time.
Time started doubling.
I started dieting so
the gap between life
and death could remain an inch.
I try not to move,
crouch under the raspberry
bush and pull its bullets off.

CALLING LATE

The men used to call
at all hours, but what I miss
most are the late-night
talks, ones where I held the phone
so close, it pressed like a gun.

TO THE RAIN

You seem so happy.
If I could be your pupil,
I would sit in front.
Please teach me how to collapse,
the way your legs break
and then spread, how you let go,
flow this way and that,
take the form of everything,
even tighten in my mouth.

LITTLE SOUL

I rode on your back
until your knees broke and now,
one mile left, I must toss you.

WHEN THE WAR IS OVER

I once saw the deer.
They were all wearing blue scarves.
We have finally finished
killing everything.
We are now looking ahead
but have killed past the future.

A DEATH IN THE DESERT

Something is slumping
over a warm rock, as if
holding its mother.
I've watched so many spiders
lift one last leg toward God.

THE DREAMERS

I sit cross-legged
in my dreams, watch people try
to touch, untouch. When
the dreams end and they wake up,
I return to the
real world. Sometimes I leave my
shoes behind. When a
person in my dream wears them,
I no longer touch the ground.

THE WILD GEESE

They are not wisdom
or freedom or history.
They are not what's lost.
They are nothing but wild geese.
I can hear them everywhere,
wings pushing down metaphor.

TO THE FACE IN THE MIRROR

Today I saw three
crows fighting on top of the
trees. I looked at myself in
the mirror. I no
longer looked like a poet.
I had a crow's face. Now I
know where all the dead birds go.

TURNING

My mother is dead.
The lemons still turn yellow,
the trout still stare emptily,
desire is still free.
We still love many people,
eat peaches as if kissing.

THE STRING

Half of the tree is
in my window, the same half
I see each weekend,
where addictions ebb and flow,
where desire is a
needle I shoot myself with.
When the earth rotates,
a person not tied down with
longing falls off into space.

RAIN AT NIGHT

To be the last drop
of rain each night is sadness.
It shuts the last door and jumps.

LARK

I have a lark in
my pocket with a broken
wing that can't fly, but
instead tries to get me to
live inside with it.
I try to turn inside out,
to bring the dead back.
But the dead are like the lark,
they won't fly or fully die.

HOW IT HAPPENS

I want to staple
myself to a passing cloud
so I am blameless for war.

SEPARATION

Each day, landscape splits
from the beauty it emits.
When nature is free
from sight, it is most
like itself. I erase each
word right after I write it.

THE SOUND OF THE LIGHT

I can't overhear
light, can't stroke it or scratch it,
can't turn it over.
It's a lot like grief, which has
ringlets of light streaked through it.

WALKERS

The walkers go by,
two by two with their heads down.
I am powerless,
separated by windows.
Everything I want
is always over there, but
when I step outside,
there are buggies and horses,
a different family inside.

WHAT IS MODERN

Mass graves are modern.
I caught up with the future—
the metal trees are silent
as they wait for us.
The future isn't modern.
It worries it won't arrive.

WHITE MORNING

An oak tree must ache,
each year of desire in rings
or maybe nothing
hurts. Maybe all pain is joy.
Maybe joy is the
flare-up to be avoided.
Don't look at the bird
on the veranda singing
nothing to us or for us.

TO THE WORDS

When the towers fell,
a branch of the oldest tree
also fell, knowing nothing.

IN THE OPEN

Weather is wet, it
doesn't have joints. How snow just
becomes rain, what's that
change called? Trees witness everything,
but they always look away.

LITTLE HORSE

No one judges it,
not even the flattered grass.
Horses are simple,
we train them and they listen.
I want so much from a horse.
It just gives me fifty years.

THE NOTES

I stay in bed and
listen for any music.
Today is cheerful,
it has overshot itself
and is tomorrow.
I'm left behind, waiting for
the birds to return.
They've moved on. I now know that
being birdless doesn't hurt.

IN THE WINTER OF MY
THIRTY-EIGHTH YEAR

All the winters came.
That winter was the last one.
Father had a stroke next year.
His brain found freedom,
tore itself out of his head,
now moves another man's mouth.

EMPTY WATER

Once I fell in love
with the most indifferent horse.
It never heard me,
only looked at me one time.
That one time lasted
forty-three years. I've lost my
speech four times, last time
was when my mother died. The
horse is still neighing for me.

LATE WONDERS

My face is now gone.
Instead, I have a hawk's face.
None of the poets
notice, they only want fame.
Fame is a bucket of eyes.

LIVES OF THE ARTISTS

I brush my hair and
wonder if you're watching.
I write a word and
attach it to a speaker—
someone please listen.
Words come out of my coffin,
made of maple. When
empty, it will return to
the trees who speak to no one.

WATCHERS

A poem is published.
It is posted everywhere.
A tree drops leaves in secret.

HOW WE ARE SPARED

The rain came last night,
gently fell down like chisels,
cut away at my
dreams until there was nothing
left but a dead girl's
lungs. Then my breathing came out
so frozen that I
had to carry a hammer
to break up all my mistakes.

TO THE HAND

Someone is turning
the earth with wrenches, each turn
a bit closer to the end.
The earth is warmer,
the crickets are still singing,
rehearsing for the last day.

THE CHILD

Every day I want to
tear off my childhood to see
if what's left survives.
If what's left dies, then I know
my childhood wasn't wasted.

LOSING A LANGUAGE

I saved Mother's words,
buried them in the ground. How
do I only kill the weeds?

FOGHORN

Sometimes the language
we have is inadequate.
On rainy days, people leave
yellow boots on the
porch. The egret takes off its
yellow feet and steals the boots.

WITNESS

From the Ferris wheel
we can see all the lovers.
We are seduced while turning.

LATE SPRING

Does spring start grieving
in April or May? Once each
spring, the girl appears
in the white house behind mine.
The window opens.
The girl paces, phone to ear.
One day I look up,
the girl is gone, window closed,
and I go back to dying.

THRESHOLD

The crows have lifted
away all the question marks.
They aren't interested
in finding truth, since they have
already seen our insides.

IT IS MARCH

In the upper leaves,
it is already next month.
I am still writing
yesterday's poems, waiting for
clarity to come.
But yesterday is clotting,
next month won't come down.
How do I live in the past
but write about tomorrow?

DISTANT MORNING

Another morning.
The trees always look the same.
I am different.
Each day, I am greedier.
How do trees refuse evening?

THE MASTER

When the moon is a
crescent, the poets are out
hunting. They worry
about insolvency, how
someone slaughters the
moon each night, its color drained,
their handprints around
the moon's neck, wringing words out.

UTTERANCE

Have you ever stood
on a highway in pitch-black
and heard nothing but singing?

THE NIGHT PLUMS

The night plums ignore
everything. They only grow
while enclosed. In that
way, we are just like plums. We
don't know who is eating us.

DIVISION

There are holes in earth,
our dead dig into soil. Their
fingers touch, dead hands
grabbing other hands. How
did they forgive each other?

COMPLETION

I am done living.
Wanting accelerates time.
When I lift the soft
grass up, I see you are bald.
So I go back to
living. But when I return,
it's a different season,
the woods are now a mall, my
children have gray hair.

THE FIRST YEAR

The year after death
is full of stretching, where things
pull so hard your bones
break, because they were never
bones, were always solitude.

THE DRAGONFLY

Out of its small mouth,
the dragonfly speaks English.
I write down each word,
but I'm disappointed. It
just tells us what it
sees—the rows of gravestones,
faceless pigeons, that
sadness is the only thing
that doesn't have a shadow.

HISTORY

History is dead.
Apricots grieve their old shape.
A dry flower can't reverse.
Some call this dying.
Those of us who live in it
know it is closer to love.

DEAD HAND

I took her hand off,
then I took my own hand off,
replaced it with hers.
My memories go around
and around her wedding ring,
forever in future tense.

TO AGE

When the stars hit the
windows now, they turn into
flies. Who knew they would come down?

SPRING

Were I to send a
cease and desist letter to
baby birds in the
rafters, their beaks would fall off.
But then the branches would die.

THE SINGER

The crickets sound like
wet flesh rubbing. They make no
sense. They may never make sense.

WHAT CAN WE CALL IT

You can't stop someone
from adding an *s* to a
word. Loves. Depressions.
Deaths. Griefs. Gods. Most of the time,
the plural of something is worse.

WORDS

I struck a bargain
with language. That I would not
abuse it or sell it, that
I would use it for
beauty. In exchange, I will
die, while words live forever.

II

Here, there are grasses rolled
into dry moons, then carted
off on trailers to the edge of
the rain. Here, there is so
much sky that even birds

get lost. Oh to be loved
the way the day loves the
night. See how slowly they
separate? All day long the
trees move, each leaf in a

different direction, as if by
the work of fingers on a body.
How many times our bodies
imagined by another mind.
How many times the day

imagined the night. Once I
loved a man so much that
when he didn't love me back,
I closed my eyes and drank
a whole bottle of night.

How I felt night rush into
my body, then out through
my skin as envelopes. At the
time I only felt pain, but years
later, all I remember is joy,

the kind of love that seems
ground off of a moon.
Perhaps such love cannot ever
be returned, except in the
imagination.

•

Today I tried to open the river. But when I pulled, the whole river disappeared. I used to think that language came from the body.

Now I know it is in that group of mountains across the field beyond the fence. Yesterday, I saw a red-tailed hawk. When I went near it, it took

the wind with it. I was left without air. But I could still breathe. I realized everything around me I could do without. I could hear the

mountains but nothing else. I saw a car start up but I heard nothing. A gray-haired woman said *hello* to me but I heard nothing. I stood and

watched the hawk. It never looked at me but knew I was there. Neither of us moved. Finally, it flew to the top of an electric pole.

I realized the pole is all the years of my life, the mountains, applause, the hawk, what I have been trying to tell myself.

•

There are so many trees here,
did someone plant them?
These trees so close to the
border look like straitjackets. I
wonder who is walking on the

expanse of dirt today, who was
walking while I was sleeping.
I felt footprints inside my
head. I felt feet jumping. I
don't understand this place

where there is no mist. Even
memory is thinner. Here,
you can pay someone to clip
off your shadow and walk it
across the border. Even the

restaurant signs use small
words, as if hiding. The desert
doesn't hide anything. In the
darkness, it quietly collects
footprints and puts them onto

the highway for others to
notice. In the morning, all the
sounds have separated from
the bodies. Everything we say
is church bells.

·

I didn't know the woman I
followed out the front door
onto the streets. Someone
had won a sports tournament.
Whatever came, came

quickly. She and I didn't speak. We ran side by side with all the others toward a center. The center had its own lungs. The center had

embryos. Blood flowers. People gathered on the street like beasts. None of them had a face. None of them spoke words. Just blood sounds,

scavenger sounds. Someone set a car on fire. Others broke windows. We stood together on the edge and watched things grow. Once I wouldn't

go into the center. Once I was 19 and flickered. Now I am 49 and still only flicker, shine behind things. The flickering now clusters, clots. But

here, in this strange place, I am running alongside no one but a shadow and I can see the lights in front of me. It is not fear. Not death. Not love. It is joy.

I still can't hold it. It still looks like a car in flames. Maybe joy is the distance that never changes and the distance is what allows me to feel it.

•

Today, I paid $30 to see art objects left over by people who are dead. They have forgotten us. Do they know they have

forgotten us? Or are they actually watching us? Once my heart sat inside the bell. It rang only when something touched it. Lately every

shadow is my dead mother. Lately the bell rings all the time but the bell is empty. Lately I have forgotten how to love the surface,

I only love the drowning. Do you see how beautiful they are? Those people without shoulders? Without hesitations? Is it possible

to stop loving everything? The owl. The hawk. Every person I meet. To see everyone as my mother. To have a heart like this

is to be made of midnight. There are always too many questions to ask and not enough time. To love so much is to live

within birds. I have been waiting for this heart to fade or at least to kneel. The heart is not inside us but we are inside it.

•

Yesterday, while looking for the owl, I met a gelding. The horse was so still that it must have been time. I almost missed it because I didn't

know I could see time. Time is the only thing that doesn't move when it moves. I stood at the fence, half hoping the horse would come over, half

hoping I was the horse. I made noises with my feet. The horse turned its head to me. *What are days for? / Days are where we live. / . . . They are to be happy*

in: / Where can we live but days? wrote Larkin. My day was this horse. This horse is all my days, with its bruises, tears, thin overworked body. I pay

all my debts to this horse. This horse is also all the hours of my life that are unlived. It is all human suffering at once. The horse knows this

and doesn't move, doesn't come near me because suffering cannot be touched. At the courthouse, a woman saw me looking up at the tree.

No owls today, she said. *Two live up there.* This whole time I had only been looking for one. One is my life and the other is what it could have been.

•

Today, when I finally left the house, I went out the back door. Something flew above my head. I looked up and saw its wings, two halves with

white tips. Nothing about the wings were about me. I used to think that everything was mine. Now I understand. Nothing is for me to take or

to decide. Neither child was interested in speaking to me, so I followed the bird I hoped was the hawk I saw the other day. I walked closer to the

tree but it flew away. I followed it and realized it was a great horned owl, the owl I had been searching for all week. It turned its head to look at me. The wind raised its feathers on one side. One side of its ear stood higher than the other. I forgot everything. I watched

the owl watch me and everything else at once. I watched nothing else. When I took a photo, the owl flew away. The owl was telling

me that taking a photo is a form of murder. Later, I posted the photo and sent it to my children. One was with friends. The other said she doesn't

care about owls. I only care about the owl. The way it doesn't seek followers. The way its face doesn't change as it moves from tree to tree.

The way it makes you think that there must be only one owl in the world and that everyone who sees an owl sees this very owl.

•

I used to ask people questions. Now the period begins everything. Here, it's always the last day, the kind of day where you least expect the egg to fall off the table. When the woman walking talks on the phone with her loud voice, I wonder whether trees find

other species annoying. Here, the river intends nothing. Not even war. I'm still waiting for water to wake up. I refuse to believe water is

dead. That things glitter because they have already died. The termites make me feel less lonely. I think of my own house and wonder

when the windows can be lifted again, when the grass can rise, when the white trucks with their packages will disappear.

Always my central question: how do we reconcile the fact that the new rain gutters are death but the rain that flows through them is life?

•

The older I get, the more I love windows, with their mornings and evenings. The more I don't understand the day. I can't erase the owl from my mind or the way it stood on the pole and let me explain myself. I told the owl I was sorry that yesterday I killed a beetle as I was

trying to move it outside. The beetle slipped off the paper as the owl flew by in my mind, lifting the paper up. I was sorry because

I once again couldn't control my mind. The beetle died right away. The owl came today because you are gone and it knew. Before you,

there were just questions but no one to ask them. Before you, there was just violence in the slab of concrete. Here, when I scream

in my own head, some of the sound leaks out. Here, when I cry in my head, my tears come out as letters. Here, I finalize the painting

of a portion of my heart. The color of paint is different from the original color, resulting in a line running down the middle. And the idea of a border emerges. The heart is now like everything else. Here, the night brings remorse. The owl brings the future. The dead beetle

brings the past. The wind brings another poet into town. And everyone here waves at me as if it's the last time they'll ever see me.

·

A Polaroid is a roundabout way of embracing time. At some point, the public contradicts painters. At some point, bodies are both religious and

nourishment. I've always liked paintings that are signs, emoting strongly. But a photograph is looking in me, laughing. It is problem-solving.

Perception between the two feels different, distorting boundaries between language and objects. Brushstrokes require faith and mistakes.

Silence operates in images. A photograph knows that the human body when activated will kill. In a painting, the body is abstract, is based on glass,

light, deconstructs viewers.
What if my images are both—
vocabulary and consciousness?
I want to work independently
and quietly, but my work is

interested in exuberance
and relationships. It needs
community, dead bodies,
wheels, beeswax, two wars,
and a queen coaxed into it.

•

Last night, there was so much
thunder that the house lost its
shape. The lightning has barely
changed. It's the same lightning
from our childhoods. I wonder

where it stores itself. I wonder
about the tornado dream
and what it is postponing. Is
nature speaking to us through
lightning, the tornado? Or are

we nature's speech? If we are
nature's speech, is anyone
listening? What if there is
nothing to say or comprehend?
What if we can't understand

because we are within nature
and can't see a thing? Today I
went to see art objects in the
desert. I felt severed from my
past. I entered the past of the

artists. They wanted me there, staring in silence, in admiration. Instead, I talked to the tour group who took me in as winter might. I could sense

their lives were near their ends. I didn't wash my hands for days. Later at dusk, I will go look again for the owls that live in the tree in front of the

courthouse. One owl flies backwards to avoid death. Someone says it's as big as a cat. There is no real road here. And I may or may not see

the owls. The thunder hasn't grown any thinner. The sky here isn't counterfeit. Elsewhere, we are all trying to speak through loudspeakers

at once. Maybe no one can hear us. Maybe no one can see us. Maybe we aren't meant to remember anything here. Just meant to see. And to forget.

III

RAIN TRAVEL

The raindrops stare back,
lined up on the window like
small faces, each drop
one second of my life. I
watch them to see which
will get too heavy and fall.
They have done their jobs.
Now in their old age,
everything said comes too late.

NOTE

A box of letters.
All the lost words are frozen,
tired of repeating themselves.

OCTOBER

Violence has been
painted over. Perhaps
violence itself can
be happy, be something
more than before or after.

THE TIME OF SHADOW

The zookeepers feed
all the shadows light and meat.
The shadows wish so
badly to leave their bodies,
but they stay for the children.

MY OTHER DARK

I imagine my
life as a Chinese empress,
proud of my face, eyes.
Even the moon has black hair,
mountaintops of Chinese snow.
In this life, I am nothing.

TRANSIT

What are words but lies?
A footnote has lost its thought.
Have you ever been
so afraid of desire, you
wished for yourself to die first?

THE PLASTER

Once, homes were made of
plaster, powdered lime, and sand,
with horsehair mixed in.
I wonder where they found the
horsehair, each home in
the middle of the night, sounds
of galloping in
walls. By morning, the horses
escape, turn into women.

DEW LIGHT

I crouch under light
to hide the minute so that
near death, I can pull it out.

THE REMOVAL

My hair falls out
as I near fifty, plus two
hundred years or more.
When my mother died, I jumped
onto a new track
made of sandstone, smooth as a
candle never lit.
There are no words here, just rain
on the nape of everything.

THAT MUSIC

Once I fell in love
with the music, not the man.
When the music played,
my heart moved like paper boats.
When it stopped, I was eighty.

INHERITANCE

I was told that we
are made of cells, but now I
think we are made of
paper and when the wind blows,
we shiver and fold
in astonishment. Men write
their dreams on us. They
like to weep on our chests. When
they're done, they use us as flint.

THE SHIPWRECK

I sit at my desk.
Desire is an anchor—
I lift it and words come up.

WATCHERS

The lemons are gone,
someone picked them off the tree.
They have grown too fast like hope.
My fingerprints are
all rubbed down from touching time.
Soon I will have lived enough.

GARDEN

Something is growing.
Plath said growing hurts at first,
but when does the hurting stop?

SEPTEMBER

This March is made of
winter and eighty-five days.
The month is bloodshot.
April should be the cruelest
month, but they are all
cruel in their inch-by-inch strike.
I take March off, put
September on like a shirt.
The months fit better than days.

THE GODS

The fact that leaves can't
be put back on trees makes me
think that you do not exist.

THE ARRIVAL

It is winter but
the poets are still coming.
I once lived in a
town where there were no poets
or children. The trees
were made of salt. When the wind
shook, nothing happened
but daylight. There were no hands
since there was nothing to take.

FOR A COMING EXTINCTION

What if we are birds?
Does that mean we also stand
on wires, tenderly, weightless.
Are we in front of
or behind the red-tailed hawk?
Which last bird must watch us die?

A DEBT

The bank is empty.
A cluster of birds live there.
The birds are all gold,
but they can fly like dollars.
They are lawless birds
glorified by all the poems.
If you look closely
at the ones in the corner,
some of them have human lips.

THE UNWRITTEN

Frost tries to silence
the field. Yesterday the grass
even strangled the mushrooms.

WANTING TO SEE

It is midwinter
and I cannot bear the minutes,
their procession as
they keep inching like snipers.
How can our purpose
be just to watch people die?
The peaches blooming
in the dark are saved for the
ground. I confess, I want them.

A DOOR

Each door that opens
could be the one where we leave
spring and its bursting behind.

THE LAUGHING THRUSH

The thrush loves no one.
Why do we keep asking it
to be our agent, to help
us read poems to
the sky? Do humans know that
the leaves aren't actually clapping?

THE HEART

Someone trimmed the tree.
Maybe there are no answers.
Small bits of blue sky through it.

THE WILD

I am still angry
with God and all the patterns
we're forced to follow.
I still can't look beyond death.
Why does the heart have
so many rivers to snake
through, each one a day's
trip, each one a suicide
mission into another.

BURNING MOUNTAIN

The fires are long gone,
but desire is left behind.
Desire was never burning.

TO IMPATIENCE

I am impatient
for the sun to rise, for it
to set, for the moon
to take off its white mask, for
the crow to start
its daily lessons on love—
how to slow it, how
to hide in its switchbacks. Why
can we love, then undo it?

THE POEM

Poets want light. The
poem is the spotlight. We can't
write poems while lit up by them.

STRAWBERRIES

Mother brought a spray
bottle to pick strawberries,
and made us spray them
before eating. I never
cared that hundreds of
red eyes watched me as I took
my first bite. They all
knew that the war had begun,
that June began the killing.

DECEMBER NIGHT

Things return at night.
Slowly the grass lifts back up.
Even the pine trees breathe out,
their blueprints open.
At night, everything rebuilds,
even violence lifts its roots.

BEGINNING

There was a first lake,
a first duck floating on top,
a first river that
knew to keep moving because
stopping meant grieving.
Lakes rely on others to
grieve, as swallows come and go.
Oceans depend on themselves,
since they collect the dead birds.

FIRST OF JUNE

Lightning is staged, rain
waits behind the tornado.
The curtain stays closed
until someone falls in love.
Then all move aside for wind.

DUSK IN WINTER

Everything is blue.
If we mend dusk, then morning
may never arrive.
At this time of day, it's hard
to tell the difference
between a rook and a star.
Snow melts on the rook's
leg. A poem is the rook's leg
only after the snow melts.

TO THE MARGIN

I will never love
anyone the way I love
my memories and their cliffs.

THE HERDS

On some nights, if you
listen closely, you can hear
the man in prison
carving letters on a wall.
If you lean in, you
can see stars being strangled
by hunting parties.
By the time the warnings come,
the earth will have one season.

BEGINNERS

The young fight the old.
The old stand on the runway,
guiding in birds who can fly.

LIVING WITH THE NEWS

The news is a fist
I can no longer open.
Sparrows are now the
same shade of blue as the sky.
Aging is watching a plane,
but only you can hear it.

UNKNOWN BIRD

All birds are unknown,
even if they have been seen.
We think we are watching them
but they are cataloging
us: children and the killers.

THE MOURNER

Standing over the
gravesite, she looks like linen.
The body below,
on its back, freshly buried,
the fingers curled hard.
When the roots of a plant die,
the plant also dies.
The woman is still standing,
like a breeze with no known source.

WAVES IN AUGUST

The waves never die.
In May, they look like reason.
They are not violent.
By August, all hope is gone,
even stars are arrested.

TALE

She is beautiful,
the workmanship of her fur.
When I think of her,
my body aches in small lights.
I want to be where
the owl is from, where a year
is four thousand days,
where there are no more countries,
where everyone gets away.

RETURNING SEASON

I still don't know if
Mother left or was taken.
I don't trust seasons,
they come to distract us from
being hunted by the moon.

TOUCHING THE TREE

How is it that trees
don't feel the way humans do?
The oldest tree is
five thousand years old, great storms
captured in its trunk.
A heart never grew inside
us. It was buried.
Its beat never meant to keep
time, just meant to keep distance.

SEARCH PARTY

I know so much now—
that mothers and fathers die,
that love is like a small wire,
that people kill deer,
that small cottages of grief
wait in the forest, smoking.

LEVIATHAN

There's a creature that
usually lives in the sea.
We brought it to land,
fed it half of our own food,
measured its wingspan,
weighed its brain, stole its nightmares,
sent it back to sea.
This is why we can drown, why
our dreams never match our lives.

THIS TIME

This moment is gone.
It cut time but left no mark.
Each day contains a thread of
joy, but joy doesn't
stitch. Our eyes look ahead while
joy travels underneath us.

GOING

What happens after?
I only know this moment,
the way four small birds
just gathered atop the tree.
The blue swallows hide.
Some come out to stalk the red
birds, the ones whose cries
sound like *look at me, look at
me.* The poems still make no sound.

RIVER SOUND REMEMBERED

How does the river
live without silence? Poets
try to hold their breath for years.

TOOL

We make tools to fix
everything—hammers, nails, wires
that we twist to hold
down or bend into beauty.
We make a small tree
into the shape we want, to
be slanted, silent.
The wire on my wrists cut-in,
I take the shape of desire.

THE SEARCH

If you give me the
exact coordinates of
my heart, I still can't
find it. Mother said that hearts
are not within our bodies.

SOME LAST QUESTIONS

Will the clock dissolve?
Did rain enjoy falling? Did
the hands truly love me? Did
the treetops know? Was
sadness what we wanted? Were
the fireflies warning us?

WORN WORDS

We collect the words,
stack them in dreams. But there were
never any words in dreams.

IN AUTUMN

It is not autumn,
it is spring. I hear the geese
who survived the trip.
Each time a bird closes its
wings, it is praying.
If I prayed that many times,
could I read the sky, what it's
trying to tell me?
Nothing known has a surface.

SHORE BIRDS

Some gulls are so smart
they use bread to catch goldfish.
They band together,
mob attackers. All this time,
I thought they were sent by God.

THE PIPER

What if there is no
piper, if no music is
coming from the hill,
if the cross is just a cross?
Then the branch is a
question from the tree, and the
hummingbird on the
branch isn't awe but a brief
answer to that question.

FATE

By the time you know
your fate, it's too late to change.
The birds in cages
know this but still chew the bars.
Maybe hope tastes like metal.

THE WELL

The well holds all the
past wars. The wind keeps blowing
smells of blood to the
bottom, stacking year by year.
War is never by
itself, just like laughter or
snow—how snowflakes take
on the scent of the bird's wing,
slip off of it as a tear.

WORLD'S END

Will earth stop spinning?
Will there only be hair left?
We are made of war—
it stays in the air,
mixed with oxygen, we breathe
it in and deploy it out.
Our birth is easy on us
but hard on everything else.

DAYLIGHT

One by one, days died,
even they weren't protected.
They have no symptoms
but keep dying. They want to
fix melancholy,
to keep coming back to no
answers, to take the
depositions of orchards.

WEST WALL

The shells are bragging,
the sand is grieving again,
it needs antidepressants.
The ocean is a
bully, always insisting
it understands hope the best.

LOOKING FOR MUSHROOMS AT SUNRISE

I have looked for them,
but I have never found them.
At sunrise I only see
things that have no weight—
the gloom of the empty homes,
inside, all the pregnant hearts.

HOMECOMING

The birds come back
but they don't tell us stories.
Their wings remember nothing,
are never knowledge.
We don't remember our birth.
When a mother dies, it's gone.

PROVISION

The field remembers
the wet boots marching on it.
The sky has scars from
birds. The body knows the square
root of desire, the cold nights
of bandaging the great fires.

IN A CLEARING

There are no lovers
in the clearing. A true muse
is someone you never had.

THE LONG AND THE SHORT OF IT

Can you remember
the very first noise you made?
The small squares on the ceiling,
the pinch of the nurse.
Memory was born with you,
then it grew into a crow.

THRESHOLD

When a country dies,
a small bell tolls on a hill,
the earth gets lighter.
Someone weighs the earth each year,
decides what to toss over.

FOR THE ANNIVERSARY OF MY DEATH

So many people
don't yet know they are not here.
I am still here in the rain,
waiting to be called.
The water is still bluish,
God is still the minute hand.

ANTIQUE SOUND

There are sounds that die—
the dodo spinning at dawn,
an arrow tip breaking skin.

BEFORE THE FLOOD

You could hear something.
Water has a head and feet,
they just change places.
Sometimes a person has three
souls that rush to the front.

PLEA FOR A CAPTIVE

Weather transfers like
currency. In some countries,
rain is worth nothing.
In others, thunder is worth
more than wind. The moon
is the cheapest. It sees us.

THE BLACK JEWEL

The black jewel is near.
Is it death or a small seed
growing inside us?
How quickly something becomes
a memory, the
thing itself is so brief that
life is mostly memory.

UNDER THE DAY

Every day I laugh,
do you hear my mouth lifting?
I fold and unfold
my heart a hundred times each
day so that it doesn't freeze.

THE WAKENING

I am cold and out
of memories. My heart is
made of snow. I fear
the coming summer, in case
it can melt all the way down.

IN A CLEARING

My whole life I thought
to mourn leaves falling. Now I
marvel at all the splitting.

APPARITIONS

There are no ghosts in
any home I've ever lived
in. Everything blurry is
me trying to escape touch.
Even the wind hurts.
I open one door and go
out the window so
nothing vanishes but me.
I withdraw my beauty twice.

THE LOVERS

There is a wildfire
starving on top of a lake.
See how the water holds fire
but cannot end it?
We insist on love
when all we want is mercy.

THE WREN

The wren is first light,
looks like a small trumpet, sings
its news here and there.
It knows we suffer and keeps
dropping its pamphlets, hoping
one day we will read them.

MIGRATION

How quickly blood moves.
When someone dies, it settles,
fills in spaces perfectly,
as if always there—
the living are trapped between
a fire and a great fire.

LEFT OPEN

We can't see beyond
the crest of the wooden gate.
We are carriers
of grass yet to be grown. We
aren't made of cells, but of fields.

A GARDEN

Inside my body,
the garden is dry and dead.
My tears have refused
to do anything but thread.
Each drop is filled with grieving.
The windows, though, still open.

PASSAGE

Every leaf that falls
never stops falling. I once
thought that leaves were leaves.
Now I think they are feeling,
in search of a place—
someone's hair, a park bench, a
finger. Isn't that
like us, going from place to
place, looking to be alive?

WITNESS

Maybe we're not filled
with water but with leaves, the
soft ones that make no
sound. If you listen closely,
you can almost hear
the leaves in your body fall.
Maybe nothing dies,
things just get lost. Memory
convalesces on our skin.

TURNING

In the fall, there are
so many choices. Red and
more red. Anything
not red seems wrong. Let me tell
you about green—how
it's really a spy, hiding
under its garment of red,
how it closes distances,
taking notes on how to leave.

IN THE DOORWAY

The fiftieth fall
is finally here. Have you
counted the number
of leaves that have brushed your face?
The number of times
fall checkmated summer? If
you think fall is made
of dying, you are wrong, it
is made up of the future.

IV

LOVE LETTERS

Is that you, crawling?
Or have you just finished
gathering our sadness?

•

Let me tell you a story
about hope: it always starts
and ends with bandages.

•

Last year had one
thousand days. Imagine all
our extra living!

•

We are made of sorrow.
It threads through us and
holds our organs together.

•

Hope has footprints too.
Some days we follow it.
Some days it follows us.

•

Don't worry. The sky isn't
really a hand. It isn't waiting to
punch you down.

•

Sadness takes time. Sadness
is made up of minutes. Hope
is made up of years.

·

All the days can feel
terrifying. Until you realize
you've done this before.

·

Do you remember where you
were last May? I do. You were
here. You were alive.

·

I learned last year that
the moon too can help
things grow.

·

Plant your sorrow in
the soil. Next year it will
grow into a set of oars.

·

If you don't forgive yourself,
tomorrow will still arrive. So you
might as well forgive yourself.

·

There's a reason why our skin
keeps out water. We each
already own enough tears.

•

If you stand near grief too
long, the pine trees might
begin to notice you.

•

Summer is coming. Do you
remember when last year we
only had one season?

•

Your heart had hundreds of
extra beats last summer. You can
use some of them this year.

•

Maybe the large hand
descending was just
a crow's wing.

•

Last year the moon was
one inch from our faces and we
thought it would never leave.

•

Some days, the animals stare
at us too long. On those days,
we don't need anything.

•

Sometimes you are the wound,
sometimes the bandage.
Last year, we were all the wound.

•

Remember the first time you
saw a spiderweb and followed
the threads to the center?

•

Don't forget what happened
last year—when you missed people
so much you let them in.

•

When grief is very
busy, it doesn't even
bother to leave.

•

It is possible to mourn grief.
One year there were so many
tears, the sea level rose.

•

Be suspicious of a happiness
that is too easy, that
is windless.

•

Sometimes even the
flowers cannot cover
the scent of grief.

•

Why spend your
life building a room
to hide in?

•

Sometimes the stranger
next to you knows you better
than you know yourself.

•

There is always someone who
loves you, just as there are
always machines everywhere.

•

Everything always dries
eventually. But this
city never dries.

•

There is a bird and a stone
in your body. Your job is not
to kill the bird with the stone.

•

Some of us are made only
of nerve endings. At night,
we light up like radium.

•

One day you will wake
up beating. One day you will
wake up winged.

•

Let me tell you a story
about hope: it always starts
and ends with birds.

I wrote a series of tankas that appeared in my prior book, *Obit.* This current book emerged from a suggestion, by a friend, to continue writing short poems. I wrote these poems in various Japanese syllabic forms called *wakas* (translated as "Japanese poem," specifically the court poetry of the sixth to fourteenth centuries in Japan) such as the katauta (5-7-7 syllable pattern), the sedoka (5-7-7-5-7-7), the tanka (5-7-5-7-7), the bussokusekika (5-7-5-7-7-7), and the choka (which can be indefinite; mine are often nine lines) (5-7-5-7-5-7-5-7-7). Sometimes the term *waka* is also used to mean a tanka. Occasionally, I broke the form.

These poems are also based on W.S. Merwin's poem titles, as a way to subconsciously avoid preconceived subject matter, in hindsight, and as a way to inhabit another person's mind. I selected Merwin's titles because of how open they seem. I selected a Merwin title as a prompt, then one syllabic form at random from the above, and then wrote a poem. I would often read the Merwin poem first, but not always.

I chose to doubly constrain myself because formal constraints often have the opposite effect on my writing process. Terrance Hayes once said in an interview, "My relationship to form is that of a bird inside of a cage, moving around."

I wrote "Marfa, Texas" during a Lannan Residency Fellowship in Marfa. The shape of the poem was inspired by my viewing of various art pieces at both the Chinati Foundation and the Judd Foundation. The section beginning "A Polaroid is a round-about way" was written as a commission for the Tang Teaching Museum and Art Gallery at Skidmore College. All words from this section are from the catalog of the Tang Museum for the *Energy in All Directions* exhibit.

The last four poems in section III ("Passage," "Witness," "Turning," and "In the Doorway") were commissioned by the Poetry Society of America and Blue Bottle Coffee, where poems were printed on coffee sleeves of its seasonal autumn single origin blend, mailed with online coffee purchases and coffee subscriptions, and shown on windows of its cafés globally.

The "Love Letters" poems were written as part of a commissioned project (*Love Letters in Light*) by the Los Angeles County Public Library and the Los Angeles County Department of Mental Health's WE RISE initiative to bring written messages of "hope, heartbreak, resilience and love" to county residents during Mental Health

Awareness Month, May 2021. The poems
(sometimes in different forms), along
with those of other artists and community
members, ran across LED light strips on
the exteriors of ten Los Angeles County
Library buildings in 2021.

ACKNOWLEDGMENTS

Thank you to the editors of the following journals in which some of the poems in this book appeared, often in earlier forms:

Academy of American Poets Poem-a-Day: "The First Year," "Late Spring," "Threshold," "Utterance," "The Wild Geese"

Air/Light: "Dusk in Winter," "Rain at Night," "Thanks," "Turning" [My mother is dead]

The American Poetry Review: "Another Year Come," "Calling Late," "A Death in the Desert," "Empty Water," "How It Happens," "Lark," "Late Wonders," "Little Soul," "To the Rain," "When the War Is Over"

Cherry Tree: "Far Along in the Story," "October"

The Cincinnati Review: "The Arrival," "For a Coming Extinction," "The Plaster," "To Impatience"

The Georgia Review: "Burning Mountain," "December Night," "Garden," "Strawberries," "The Wild"

Harvard Review: "Migration," "The Wren"

Hunger Mountain Review: "The Black Jewel," "In the Open," "Under the Day"

Los Angeles Review of Books: "A Debt," "What Is Modern"

Michigan Quarterly Review: "The Shipwreck"

Mississippi Review: "The Well," "World's End"

The Nation: "The Notes"

New England Review: "Marfa, Texas: Here, there are grasses rolled," "Marfa, Texas: Today, I paid $30 to see art," "Marfa, Texas: Today I tried to open the river" (all published as "Marfa, Texas")

The New Republic: "In a Clearing" [There are no lovers], "My Other Dark," "Provision," "Transit"

Plume: "The Mourner," "Waves in August"

A Public Space: "First of June," "The Heart"

The Sewanee Review: "Homecoming," "Marfa, Texas: I didn't know the woman I," "Marfa, Texas: There are so many trees here" (both published as "Marfa, Texas"), "The Piper," "River Sound Remembered"

The Shanghai Literary Review: "The Dragonfly, "History" [History is dead], "Plea for a Captive," "To Age"

Southeast Review: "The Gods," "Lives of the Artists"

VIDA Review: "Convenience," "Foghorn," "Green Fields," "Witness" [From the Ferris wheel]

Virginia Quarterly Review: "Gift," "History" [Today is circling], "No One," "Orioles," "Passing," "Rain Light," "The River of Bees," "Separation," "The Sound of the Light," "The Thread"

The Yale Review: "Avoiding News by the River," "Still Morning," "To Ashes," "To the Book," "When You Go Away," "White Morning"

"Marfa, Texas: Today I tried to open the river" was published in *The Best American Poetry 2021* (as "Marfa, Texas"), edited by Tracy K. Smith, published by Scribner.

Thanks to Copper Canyon Press. Thanks to Milkweed Editions and to the many other editors who have supported my writing over the years.

Thanks to the Lannan Foundation for the gift of a Lannan Residency. Thank you to the Judd Foundation. Thanks also to the Chinati Foundation for giving me a private tour.

Thanks to all my friends and supporters, especially Ilya Kaminsky. Thanks

also to G.C. Waldrep, Dana Levin, Rick
Barot, Paisley Rekdal, Mark Wunderlich,
Dean Rader, Maggie Smith, Ada Limón,
Matthew Zapruder, Ismail Muhammad,
Elline Lipkin, Nan Cohen, Jaswinder
Bolina, Wayne Miller, Ann Townsend,
David Baker, Liza Voges, Sarah Chalfant,
Jen Chang, Brian Teare, Cecily Parks,
Cyrus Cassells, Dan Handler, the late Jon
Tribble, and my entire Saturday morning
poetry group, and so many more. I'm sure
I've missed people and for that, I'm sorry.
Thanks to my family and wiener dogs
Mustard and Ketchup for always support-
ing me.

Victoria Chang's latest poetry book is *Obit,*
published by Copper Canyon Press in 2020.
Obit was named a *New York Times* Notable
Book and received the Los Angeles Times
Book Prize, the Anisfield-Wolf Book Award,
and the PEN Voelcker Award. It was also
longlisted for a National Book Award and a
finalist for the National Book Critics Circle
Award and the Griffin International Poetry
Prize. Her nonfiction hybrid book, *Dear
Memory,* was published in 2021 by Milkweed
Editions. She has received a Guggenheim
Fellowship and lives in Los Angeles, where
she serves as the program chair of Antioch's
low-residency MFA Program.

Lannan Literary Selections

For two decades Lannan Foundation has supported
the publication and distribution of exceptional
literary works. Copper Canyon Press gratefully
acknowledges their support.

LANNAN LITERARY SELECTIONS 2022

Chris Abani, *Smoking the Bible*

Victoria Chang, *The Trees Witness Everything*

Nicholas Goodly, *Black Swim*

Dana Levin, *Now Do You Know Where You Are*

Michael Wasson, *Swallowed Light*

RECENT LANNAN LITERARY SELECTIONS FROM COPPER CANYON PRESS

Mark Bibbins, *13th Balloon*

Sherwin Bitsui, *Dissolve*

Jericho Brown, *The Tradition*

Victoria Chang, *Obit*

Leila Chatti, *Deluge*

Shangyang Fang, *Burying the Mountain*

June Jordan, *The Essential June Jordan*

Laura Kasischke, *Lightning Falls in Love*

Deborah Landau, *Soft Targets*

Rachel McKibbens, *blud*

Philip Metres, *Shrapnel Maps*

Aimee Nezhukumatathil, *Oceanic*

Paisley Rekdal, *Nightingale*

Natalie Scenters-Zapico, *Lima :: Limón*

Natalie Shapero, *Popular Longing*

Frank Stanford, *What About This:
Collected Poems of Frank Stanford*

Arthur Sze, *The Glass Constellation:
New and Collected Poems*

Fernando Valverde, *America* (translated by Carolyn Forché)

Matthew Zapruder, *Father's Day*

Poetry is vital to language and living. Since 1972, Copper Canyon Press has published extraordinary poetry from around the world to engage the imaginations and intellects of readers, writers, booksellers, librarians, teachers, students, and donors.

COPPER CANYON PRESS WISHES TO EXTEND A SPECIAL THANKS TO THE FOLLOWING SUPPORTERS WHO PROVIDED FUNDING DURING THE COVID-19 PANDEMIC:

4Culture
Academy of American Poets (Literary Relief Fund)
City of Seattle Office of Arts & Culture
Community of Literary Magazines and Presses (Literary Relief Fund)
Economic Development Council of Jefferson County
National Book Foundation (Literary Relief Fund)
Poetry Foundation
U.S. Department of the Treasury Payroll Protection Program

WE ARE GRATEFUL FOR THE MAJOR SUPPORT
PROVIDED BY:

THE PAUL G. ALLEN
FAMILY FOUNDATION

The poems are set in Minion Pro.
Book design and composition by Phil Kovacevich.